EAT FOR YOUR GUT

By Dr. Nicole Rivera

EAT FOR YOUR
CONDITION
A COOKBOOK SERIES

Website: www.eatforyourgut.com
Cover + Book Design by Rachel Pesso
Cover Photographs by Charleen Artese
Food Photographs by Dr. Nicole Rivera

ISBN-13: 978-1532780783
ISBN-10: 1532780788

Table of Contents

WHO AM I?

My name is Dr. Nicole Rivera, I am the owner of Integrative Wellness Group and a practicing Functional Medicine Doctor. My wellness journey started a long time ago. I grew up in an Italian household with Sunday pasta dinners and an obsession with breaded chicken cutlets that I demanded for lunch as a preschooler.

When I was young, I didn't learn too much about cooking. However, I picked up on a few family recipes like making a mean tomato sauce or what Italian Americans affectionately call "gravy." I started working in the restaurant industry at 15 years old where I really started to expand my knowledge of food and palette for ethnic cuisine. One of my most transformational jobs was at a high end restaurant in Philadelphia where I learned a lot about what I call "fancy food." The restaurant prided themselves on sourcing fresh, whole foods indigenous to the Positano Coast of Italy.

I will never forget the day a customer demanded we add chicken parmesan to the menu and my boss (straight off the boat from Italy) stormed in the kitchen and started cursing in Italian. While laughing, I inquired why on Earth she was losing it. She informed me that chicken parmesan does not exist in Italy, because their culture is all about amazing, fresh fish with simple ingredients like lemon and olive oil.

That moment was so pivotal for me. I realized there were so many cultures around the world enjoying delicious, homemade foods that did not come from a package or a fryer, which was primarily Standard American Diet (SAD).

I decided to play with my mom's recipes and "healthify" them. I was successful at it, but still did not have a large knowledge base of healthy cooking. After college, I moved to California for chiropractic school where I learned about healthy living, organic food, GMO's, and toxins, which was where my cooking went to the next level.

I always had a passion for food. Every dollar I saved in college went towards swanky dinners in San Francisco. My best friend – also a food lover and fantastic cook – and I talked about opening a restaurant as a retirement plan. Keep in mind, we haven't even started our careers yet. During school, I was obsessed with nutrition classes, but I focused on becoming a good chiropractor since that was the whole reason I moved to Cali in the first place.

I started practicing in Seattle, WA. My office was next to the Microsoft building, which made up most of our clientele. Our office was strictly chiropractic and did not offer nutritional services. As a new practitioner, I can't even count how many clients came in stating that they were not feeling better from the adjustment.

I was so frustrated, because it had nothing to do with the quality of my body work, and everything to do with their lifestyle. I was working on people who worked 15 hour days, drank tons of coffee, and ate out of a vending machine. No chiropractic adjustment could magically undo all that damage.

So, I decided to offer nutritional services along with chiropractic care in my own practice. My fiancé and I moved to NJ in 2011 to open Integrative Wellness Group in Belmar, New Jersey. Our mission was to help people get well and stay well through various facets of healing.

I started my nutritional services based on simple blood and hair analysis to better guide my clients. I then embarked on a functional medicine degree, which expanded my knowledge base and understanding of how certain foods affect certain conditions. I created recipes and meal plans to heal specific ailments. Then, I had a light bulb moment to write a cookbook to help people to heal and manage their conditions, and enjoy awesome food while doing it! From my kitchen to yours, bon appetit!

WHY AM I EATING FOR MY GUT?

This cookbook will empower you to take control of your health and use food to improve your current condition. My recipes are geared toward an easy-to-digest, anti-inflammatory diet that can help you relieve any gastrointestinal discomfort you may have. There are many layers to gut health. Diet is obviously a very important one, but there is also the possibility of an overgrowth of bacteria, yeast, or infestation of parasites. If you try upgrading your diet and your symptoms do not improve, see a Functional Medicine doctor in your area for proper analysis to understand your symptoms. Functional Medicine doctors use specific analysis such as stool analysis, neurotransmitter testing, heavy metal testing, blood testing, and autoimmune testing for a more accurate diagnosis.

Eating for your gut will help people eliminate foods that inflame and irritate the gastrointestinal system which will decrease digestive issues and abdominal discomfort. The foods incorporated in these recipes are geared toward cleansing the gut, repairing its integrity, and replenishing the good flora for healthy digestion and elimination. Healing the gut depends on your current symptoms and/or current diagnosis. This book creates a guide for those dealing with an autoimmune condition and those who are struggling with dysbiosis. Dysbiosis is an imbalance in the gut flora resulting in symptoms like constipation, diarrhea, bloating, gas, reflux, heartburn, and abdominal pain or cramping.

Autoimmunity is typically associated with some level of dysbiosis, but also has another component known as leaky gut syndrome. Leaky gut is when the integrity of the gut lining becomes compromised and foreign particles can pass more easily from the gut into the bloodstream.

In a healthy gut, only nutrients can pass into the blood. This leakiness can happen due to toxins, pesticides, heavy metals, and genetically modified foods that damage the gut lining. When foreign particles like bacteria, yeast, or food particles get into the bloodstream where they are unwelcome, the immune system will react.

> There were so many cultures around the world enjoying delicious, homemade foods that did not come from a package or a fryer, which was primarily Standard American Diet (SAD).

Your immune system kicks in an inflammatory response to foods like gluten, dairy, eggs, and nightshades (ie. tomatoes, white potatoes, peppers, and eggplant). Your body will soon create a memory of these invaders through the production of antibodies. Your body will actually remember that these foods are foreign invaders and that they need to be attacked upon entering the body. This speaks to people who have food sensitivities, food allergies, and/or autoimmune conditions.

In autoimmunity, the memory component of the immune system can have a level of error. As the immune system attacks these foreign invaders, sometimes the immune system can confuse organ tissue for the foreign invader, which can allow an attack on an organ. Since some hybridized foods like gluten have been known to have protein sequences that resemble the tissue that makes up the thyroid, overconsumption over the long term can trigger an attack of the thyroid.

There are many other factors that play into autoimmunity such as heavy metals, toxicity, and stress, but our focus is on foods that heal the gut to take you off of the autoimmune spectrum. The point to be made here is when eating for autoimmunity, you want to eliminate all inflammatory foods and heal your gut. You must heal the gut before focusing on the organ that is being affected by the autoimmune attack.

One disclaimer: If you embark on changing your diet and hit a plateau with feeling better, you may need testing for bacteria, parasites, or yeast overgrowth. Depending on how overgrown or dysbiotic the gut may be, you may require supplement intervention to help you heal.

One of the features of my cookbook is using bone broth while cooking. The idea of bone broth goes back to Grandma making chicken soup when you were sick. The chicken stock was made from simmering the bones of the chicken.

The building blocks of the broth were calcium, magnesium, and bone marrow which are amazing for the immune system. Bone marrow is comprised of white blood cells, red blood cells, and platelets. White blood cells are an essential part of your immune system since they combat infection. Platelets allow your body to clot and heal from injuries or wounds. When you consume the bone marrow stock, you receive immune boosting benefits, trace minerals, healthy blood support, and healing benefits. In this day and age, chicken soup from a can serves has little to no health benefits.

The other component of bone marrow stock is its ability to heal the gut lining. Essentially, bone marrow is rich with stem cells. Stem cells are used as a medical intervention to rebuild healthy cells of organs and other tissues. When drinking a stock chock full of bone marrow, you heal your GI system. It is a great tool for decreasing leaky gut syndrome.

SEE PAGE 141 FOR THE ORIGINAL BONE BROTH RECIPE

Drinkable Turmeric Bone Broth

4-2 inch nubs of bones

2 tsp of apple cider vinegar

1-2 inch nub of ginger

1-2 inch nub of turmeric

2 full lemons for juice

Salt + Pepper to taste

80 ounces of water

Directions:

Heat the oven to 400F. Season the bone marrow with salt and place onto a bake pan. Bake for 10 minutes or until marrow is bubbly. Place bones into a stockpot with 80 ounces of water. Add the apple cider vinegar, spices, peeled turmeric, and peeled ginger. Allow to simmer for 4-5 hours or until marrow is soft. Use a slotted spoon to remove the ginger and turmeric root and add to a blender. Add the lemon juice to the blender and blend until smooth. Add the paste to the broth and mix. Bone broth is normally chunky. You can use an immersion blender to make it smooth, if desired.

Cooking Guides

DEFINITIONS

Conventional – Conventional oils are typically not organic and contain pesticides.

Unrefined – Unrefined oils are typically raw and natural because they are not processed to remove impurities.

Refined – Refined oils are processed to remove certain elements.

Hydrogenated – Hydrogenated oils are typically genetically modified and have a forced chemical addition of hydrogen in order to make certain foods hard at room temperature. The more hydrogen atoms, the less permeable (allowing things to pass through) the cell wall is, which blocks the food from providing proper nutrition. This also causes hardening of the cell wall which increasing aging.

Saturated Fats – Saturated fats are best for hot uses such as cooking because they have a higher smoke point.

Unsaturated Fats – Unsaturated fats are best for cold uses since they are easily damaged/oxidized when heat is applied to them.

Trans Fats – Trans fats are unsaturated fats that have gone through hydrogenation. They are damaging to your cells and increase aging.

WHAT TO USE:

High in Omega-3 and Should Not be Heated
+ Flax (unrefined) – if possible buy flax from stores that refrigerate them
+ Hemp (unrefined) - if possible buy hemp from stores that refrigerate them; contains GLA, the only Omega-6 with anti-inflammatory properties
+ Walnut (refined) – heavily refined at high temperatures, which may compromise the Omega-3s; better to use raw walnuts on a salad

High in Monounsaturated Fats and should only be heated to a low heat
+ Safflower (high oleic; unrefined)
+ Hazelnut (unrefined)
+ Olive – very low in Omega-6, high in flavonoids
+ Macadamia – contains unique antioxidants
+ Avocado (unrefined/raw) – high in "good" fats, but you're still better off eating an avocado
+ Almond (unrefined)

Neutral Fats that can be heated to a medium heat
+ Coconut (unrefined) – high in "good" saturated fat and low in Omega-6; buy virgin and unrefined

High in Monounsaturated Fats and can be heated to high heats
+ Lard (non-hydrogenated)
+ Duck Fat
+ Butter (grass-fed) – source of conjugated Linoleic Acid (good) and low in Omega-6
+ Grass Fed Ghee – clarified butter: butterfat with the milk fat removed; has a higher smoke point therefore preferred in certain cooking methods and has a longer shelf-life.
+ Beef Tallow (grass fed)

WHAT TO AVOID:

High in "Bad" Saturated or Trans Fats which hardens cells and speeds up aging
+ Beef Tallow (grain-fed)
+ Margarine (hydrogenated)
+ Coconut (hydrogenated)
+ Shortening (always hydrogenated)
+ Canola (conventional) – genetic modification
+ Rice Oil & Rice Bran Oil
+ Sunflower (linoleic; refined)
+ Safflower (refined)

High in Omega-6 which is inflammatory
+ Pumpkin Seed (refined)
+ Sesame (refined)
+ Grapeseed
+ Soybean – genetic modification
+ Cottonseed – genetic modification
+ Corn – genetic modification
+ Palm & Palm Kernel – genetic modification
+ Butter (grain-fed)

ASK YOUR FARMER

When food shopping, you want to ensure you are purchasing high quality, natural, and whole foods. The best way to guarantee this is by ASKING QUESTIONS. Here are some of the basic questions you should be asking your local farmers.

Questions to ask your farmer, butcher, or grocery store...

When purchasing BEEF or other types of RED MEAT
You want the cows to be raised outdoors and free roaming on the pasture. Cows should be grass fed for their whole lives, so when seeking quality beef you want grass fed and grass finished beef. You also want the animals to be raised without antibiotics or hormones.

+ Are your cows raised on pasture?
+ What do you feed your cows?
+ Are your cows finished on grain or in a feedlot?
+ Have your cows ever been given antibiotics?
+ Are your cows given any form of growth promoters?

When purchasing POULTRY and EGGS
You want the chickens to be raised outdoors and free roaming on the pasture. Chickens should eat a Non GMO diet, so don't be fooled by "vegetarian diet".
You also want the animals to be raised without antibiotics or hormones.

+ Are your chickens/turkeys raised on pasture, indoors, or confined?
+ On a daily basis, how much time do your chickens/turkeys spend outdoors?
+ What do you feed your chickens/turkeys? Do you feed them GMO grain or corn?
+ Have your chickens/turkeys ever been given antibiotics?
+ Are you chickens/turkeys given any form of growth promoters?

When purchasing HOGS

You want pigs and hogs to be raised outdoors and free roaming on the pasture. You want to seek out Heritage Pork which is a cleaner source of pork. You also want the animals to be raised without antibiotics or hormones.

+ Are your hogs raised on pasture, indoors, with proper bedding?
+ Are your hogs born on your farm?
+ On a daily basis, how much time do your hogs spend outdoors?
+ What do you feed your hogs?
+ Have your hogs ever been given antibiotics?
+ Are your hogs ever given any type of hormones or food additives?

When purchasing SEAFOOD

You always want your fish to be wild caught. Farm raised fish are high in toxins due to their diet of genetically modified corn and grain. Fish will tend to develop parasites when eating a corn and grain diet. Fish farmed in the ocean are advertised to be a healthy sustainable option but these fish are still consuming a poor diet. You also want to be aware of where the fish is coming from. There are many polluted bodies of water near industrialized areas and parts of Asia.

+ Is the fish Wild or Farm Raised?
+ Where was the fish sourced?

When purchasing FRUITS/VEGETABLES

You want to avoid all produce that have been contaminated with pesticides, herbicides, and fertilizers. You also want to avoid genetically modified crops. The most common being corn, soy, wheat, cotton (cottonseed oil), and sugar beets.

+ Who grows the fruits and vegetables?
+ Where is the farm located and how large is it?
+ Are any pesticides, herbicides, or fertilizers used on the crops?
+ Is the farm diversified, growing a large variety of vegetables and fruits?
+ Are any of the varieties genetically engineered?

SPICES *Your new medicine cabinet*

Everything
+ Garlic Powder
+ Onion Powder
+ Himalayan Salt
+ Truffle Salt
+ Ground Pepper
+ Black Lava Salt
+ Sea Salt
+ Cayenne
+ Turmeric
+ Thyme
+ Rosemary

Sweets/Baking
+ Mexican Vanilla Extract
+ Ceylon Cinnamon
+ Mayan Cocoa: Cocoa, Chiles, Cinnamon
+ Mexican Vanilla Powder
+ Cloves
+ Nutmeg
+ Cacao Powder: unprocessed cocoa
+ Organic Turbinado Sugar

Asian
+ Ground Ginger
+ Tamarind Extract
+ Black Sesame Seeds
+ Kaffir Lime Leaves

Middle Eastern: Many Blends mixed with coconut cream or milk to make sauce
+ Cardamom
+ Cinnamon
+ Turmeric
+ Lemongrass powder
+ Ginger
+ Kaffir lime leaves,
+ Paprika
+ Cloves
+ Ground Coriander
+ Dill Weed

Italian
+ Fresh or Dry Oregano
+ Fresh Basil
+ Fresh or Dry Sage
+ Truffle Salt
+ Fennel Seeds

Spanish
+ Smoked Spanish Paprika
+ Saffron
+ Granulated Onion
+ Granulated Garlic
+ Parsley
+ Thyme
+ Rosemary
+ Cumin
+ Arrowroot

Mexican
+ Ground Chipotle Peppers
+ Paprika
+ Urfa Chiles (Mild)
+ Chili Powder
+ Cumin

Seasoning Blends

+ **Adobo:** Spanish Paprika, Salt, Pepper, Oregano, Arrowroot, Cumin, Onion, Cloves

+ **Lemon Grass Curry:** Green Chiles, lemongrass powder, shallots, salt, garlic, onion, lampong peppercorns, galangal, ginger, kaffir lime leaves, ref thai chilis.

+ **Harissa Spice:** Japone Peppers, cumin, cayenne, coriander, paprika, garlic, salt, carway.

+ **Rogan Josh:** Paprika, garlic, ginger, coriander, cumin, turmeric, cayenne, Saigon cinnamon, cardamom, cloves.

+ **Moroccan Seasoning:** paprika, sugar, cumin, salt, Ceylon cinnamon, black cardamom, parsley, coriander, turmeric.

+ **Fennel Rub:** sugar, salt, orange peel, coriander, California paprika, ground fennel, granulated onion, granulated garlic, fennel pollen and Amarillo chiles.

+ **Charcoal Rub:** Salt, garlic, onion, black pepper, activated charcoal, cumin, Mediterranean thyme, chipotle, Greek oregano, hickory smoke flavoring.

+ **Honey Mustard Rub:** Salt, Pepper, Honey Powder, Ground Mustard, Turmeric, Granulated Onion, Granulated Garlic, Cumin, Coriander.

+ **BBQ Rub:** Salt, Granulated garlic, Brown Sugar, Granulated Onion, Paprika, Ground Mustard, Cayenne.

+ **Taco Seasoning:** Ground Chiles, Tomato Powder, Granulated Garlic, Paprika, Cumin, Granulated Onion, Brown Sugar, Mexican Oregano, and All Spice.

Fresh Organic Herbs
+ Basil
+ Thai Basil
+ Oregano
+ Sage
+ Cilantro
+ Parsley
+ Rosemary
+ Thyme

EQUIPMENT GUIDE

ICE TRAY

MANDOLINE

VITAMIXER

IMMERSION BLENDER

GRATER

WHISK

PEELER

CITRUS JUICER

MICROPLANE

SAUTE PAN

SAUCE POT

BAKING SHEET

BAKING DISH

GARLIC PRESS

VEGGETI

CHAPTER 01

GI Dysbiosis Recipes

Dysbiosis is an imbalance in the gut flora resulting in symptoms like constipation, diarrhea, bloating, gas, reflux, heartburn, and abdominal pain or cramping.

What Causes Dysbiosis?

+ Candida or Other Yeast Overgrowth
+ Overuse of Antibiotics or Steroid Hormones
+ Bacterial Infection of the Colon
+ Bacterial Infection of the Stomach: H. Pylori
+ Parasites
+ SIBO: Small Intestine Bacterial Overgrowth
+ Associated Conditions: Chronic Fungal Infections, Yeast Infections, & Urinary Tract Infections
+ Skin Conditions: Eczema, Acne, Hives. See Autoimmune for Psoriasis
+ If skin does not improve, use the Autoimmune Recipes

What does it look like?

+ Constipation
+ Diarrhea
+ Chronic Loose Bowel Movements
+ Bloating
+ Gas
+ Burping
+ Indigestion
+ Sinus Congestion or Sinusitis
+ Sinus Headaches
+ Feeling Puffy aka Inflamed
+ Yeast Infections
+ Urinary Tract Infections
+ Eczema
+ Rosacea
+ Hives
+ Itchy Skin

Eat It:

+ Probiotic Rich Foods: Fermented Kimchi, Fermented Sauerkraut, Goat's Milk Yogurt
+ Anti-Fungal and Anti-Microbial Foods: Rutabaga, Garlic, Onion, Lemon, Lime, Cilantro, Parsley, Turmeric, Coconut Oil, Ginger
+ High Quality Fats: Olive Oil, Coconut Oil, Grass Fed Ghee, Pasture Raised Grass Fed Butter
+ Pit Fruits: Mango and Avocados
+ Quality, Pasture Raised Chicken
+ Grass Fed Grass Finished Red Meats
+ White Fish: Cod, Scrod, Flounder, Mahi Mahi, Sea Bass, Striped Bass, Rockfish
+ Fresh, Organic Vegetables

Don't Eat It:

+ Wheat & Wheat Gluten
+ Oatmeal
+ Gluten Free Grains: Oats, Quinoa, Brown Rice, Wild Rice, Millet, Amaranth, Buckwheat, Spelt, Kamut
+ Refined Sugars & Artificial Sugars
+ Fruit: Limit to 1 Serving Per Day ie. 1 Cup of Berries or ½ Banana
+ Corn
+ Shellfish: Especially Shrimp
+ Soy: Soy Milk, Soy Oil, Tempeh, or Tofu
+ Limit Legumes: Black Beans, Garbanzo Beans, Cannellini Beans, Peanuts

If you suspect yeast: no chocolate, wine, vinegar, and mushrooms (except shitake)

Breakfast Time

INGREDIENTS

2 sardines, fresh is preferred

¼ white onion, sliced

6 sprigs fresh parsley, chopped

2 garlic cloves, chopped

Himalayan salt

Fresh ground pepper

¼ tsp garlic powder

1 tsp ghee

Dash of turmeric

4 eggs

Mazi Piri Piri hot sauce (optional)

DIRECTIONS

In a sauté pan, heat ghee to a medium heat. Add garlic, onion, sardines, parsley, salt, pepper, garlic powder, and turmeric. Cook for 5 minutes then remove from the pan and place in a bowl.

Cook eggs to your liking and place them overtop sardine mixture. Top with hot sauce (optional).

INGREDIENTS

½ lb. sunchokes aka Jerusalem Artichokes (approx. 6 sunchokes)

3 artichokes

3 sprigs of parsley

1 tip of capers

2 tsp. of Olive oil

3 tbsp. of veggie broth

Salt

Pepper

Turmeric

3 pasture raised eggs

DIRECTIONS

Preheat oven to 400 degrees.

Heat the olive oil to a medium heat in a sauté pan. Sauté Sunchokes, artichokes, parsley, and capers in olive oil. Add broth and cover to cook sunchokes until tender. Season to your liking.

Place mixture into an oven safe bowl and top with 3 egg yolks and bake for 10 minutes or cook eggs stovetop to your liking and serve with homefries.

INGREDIENTS

¼ lb. ground chicken

¾ lb. ground veal

½ onion

6 garlic cloves, crushed or chopped

3 large sage leaves, chopped

2 tsp. Ghee

Salt and pepper to taste

DIRECTIONS

Heat ghee in a saucepan to a medium heat. In a bowl mix together all ingredients. Make mixture into patties and pan sear them with ghee until brown.

Creamy Eggs with Zest

INGREDIENTS

2 whole eggs, per person

1 tbsp. Bone broth per egg

2 cloves of garlic, chopped

2 tsp. Grass fed ghee

½ lemon, for zest

½ lime, for zest

Drizzle of Olive oil

1 tbsp. crushed raw almonds for every 2 eggs

Salt

Pepper

Garlic powder

DIRECTIONS

Heat the ghee in a saucepan on medium heat. Place garlic into warm ghee for one minute. In a bowl, mix eggs with spices and bone broth. Add mixture to a pan with melted ghee. Eggs can be cooked either scrambled or omelet style.

Place cooked eggs into a bowl and drizzle olive oil over top. Grate lemon and lime zest over top of the eggs.

Add 1 tbsp. of crushed almonds per two eggs over top eggs.

Cauliflower Frittata

INGREDIENTS

1 head cauliflower, chopped into florets

¼ cup fresh basil, chopped

4-5 garlic cloves, crushed

1 white onion, chopped

2 tsp salt

Fresh ground pepper

1 tsp garlic powder

6 eggs

DIRECTIONS

Preheat oven to 375 degrees.

Place cauliflower florets into the blender or food processor to chop into a rice consistency. Place cauliflower, onion, basil, and garlic into a large bowl.
Season with salt, pepper, and garlic powder.

Mix all ingredients together well before adding to a medium sized Pyrex bake pan.

In a separate bowl, beat the eggs and then pour over the cauliflower mixture.
Bake for 20 minutes, or until the eggs are firm.

TIP: Use additional eggs if the 6 do not coat all of the cauliflower.

Lunch
Time

INGREDIENTS

Prep Note: Make Anchovy Vinaigrette using recipe from Sauces, Spreads, & Marinades section.

4 cups of olive leaf lettuce

Himalayan salt

Fresh black pepper

¼ cup of the Anchovy Vinaigrette

DIRECTIONS

Prep: Prepare the Anchovy Vinaigrette from "Sauces and Marinades Section".

In a large salad bowl add olive leaves, anchovy vinaigrette dressing, and salt and pepper to taste. Gently toss salad to coat all ingredients with dressing. Top with protein if desired.

Dijon Tuna Steak Salad

INGREDIENTS

2 lbs of tuna steak
1 avocado
2 garlic cloves
Juice from ½ a lemon
3 tsp of Dijon mustard
2 celery stalks, chopped
3 green onion stalks, chopped
2 tsp of capers

DIRECTIONS

Heat ghee to a medium heat in a sauté pan for searing the tuna. Pan sear the tuna for 3-4 minutes on each side. Mix the avocado and Dijon mustard with salt and pepper in a mixing bowl until smooth. Chop the tuna steak into cubes. Place tuna, green onion, celery, and capers into the bowl with the avocado and Dijon mustard and mix until fully coated.

INGREDIENTS

2 golden beets, thinly sliced

½ radicchio head, thinly sliced

1 celery stalk, thinly sliced

½ fennel bulb, thinly sliced

Juice from 1 lemon

¼ cup olive oil

1 tsp apple cider vinegar or red wine vinegar

Salt and pepper to taste

DIRECTIONS

Slice the beets, celery, and fennel with a mandolin, if possible. Otherwise, slice as thin as possible with a knife. Place all sliced vegetables in a large bowl and add olive oil, vinegar, lemon, salt, and pepper. Mix together well, until all vegetables are coated.

INGREDIENTS

6 oz. cooked salmon

3 cups lettuce

¼ avocado, diced

1 grapefruit or 1 large blood orange

1 small red onion, thinly sliced

DIRECTIONS

Pre-heat the oven to 375F. Place the salmon on a bake safe pan and season with salt and pepper. Bake for 12-15 minutes or until cooked.

In a large bowl combine lettuce, avocado, grapefruit or orange, and onion. Drizzle dressing over top the salad and toss well. Top with the cooked salmon filet.

INGREDIENTS

1 ½ lbs. chicken breast

3 scallions, chopped

1 garlic clove, crushed

1 Carrot, shredded

2 celery stalks, chopped thin

2-3 tsp Dijon mustard

1 tsp olive oil

Juice of ½ lemon

Salt and pepper to taste

DIRECTIONS

Preheat oven to 375 degrees.

On a baking pan place chicken breasts, drizzle with olive oil and season with salt and pepper. Roast in oven for 15-20 minutes. When fully cooked, remove it from the oven and chop chicken into cubes.

Place chicken, scallions, carrots, celery, and garlic in a bowl.
Add mustard, olive oil, lemon juice, salt and pepper. Mix until fully coated.

INGREDIENTS

5 large chicken cutlets

1 garlic clove, minced

2 tsp of Dijon mustard

3 green onion stalks, chopped

2 carrots, shaved with peeler

2 celery stalks, chopped

4 tsp of balsamic Vinegar

¼ cup olive oil

2 tbsp. parsley, chopped

DIRECTIONS

Preheat oven to 375 degrees.

Season chicken cutlets with salt and pepper and place on a baking pan with ghee. Roast in the oven for 20 minutes. Once finished allow to cool for 5 minutes.

While cooking, in a blender or Vitamixer, place garlic, Dijon mustard, and balsamic vinegar and blend until smooth.

In a bowl, add chopped green onions, carrots, celery, and parsley and pour the balsamic mixture over top.

Chop the roasted chicken into cubes and add it to the bowl. Mix all ingredients together well.

INGREDIENTS

1 pint cherry tomatoes, cut in half

1 ½ cups Kalamata olives

3 artichoke hearts, quartered (12 pieces)

1 orange bell pepper, chopped

½ cucumber, chopped

½ red onion, chopped

1 avocado, chopped

Juice of 1 lemon

¼ cup olive oil

1 tsp oregano

Salt and pepper to taste

DIRECTIONS

Place all ingredients into a large salad bowl. Mix together well, until the avocado breaks down a bit, and the olive oil and lemon juice are incorporated. Can serve immediately or after chilled.

Vinegar Pepper Wings

INGREDIENTS

2 lbs. organic chicken wings

1 jar pepperoncini's, chopped

1 jar hot cherry peppers

3 tsp grass fed butter

3 tsp hot sauce

Olive oil

Salt and pepper to taste

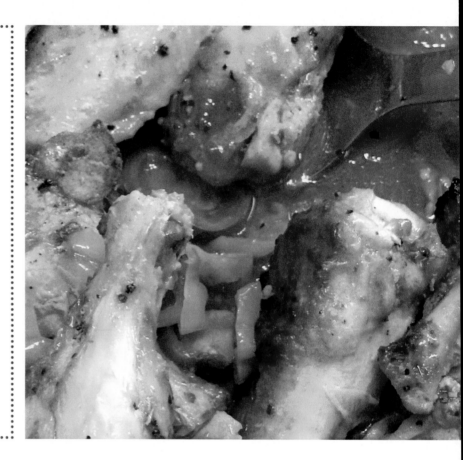

DIRECTIONS

Preheat oven to 375 degrees.

Place the wings on a baking sheet then drizzle olive oil over top. Season with salt and pepper and cook in oven for 30 minutes.

After 30 minutes, put the oven on broil and cook for another 3-5 minutes or until wings are browned.

Remove the wings from the baking sheet and place in a large cast iron pan or an oven safe pan. Pour the hot cherry peppers and the pepperoncini's over top the wings, including the juice. Add hot sauce and butter and place wings back into the oven for an additional 10 minutes.

Dinner
Time

INGREDIENTS

50 whole garlic cloves

1 medium onion, chopped

3 cups vegetable broth (can use more or less depending on your desired thickness)

2 tbsp. coconut oil

Juice from ½ lemon

Salt and pepper to taste

Makes approximately 4 small portions

DIRECTIONS

Preheat oven to 365 degrees.

In a baking dish melt coconut oil then place all of the garlic cloves and chopped onion into dish. Season with salt and pepper, and place in oven. Bake for 45 minutes or until garlic becomes lightly browned and soft.

When finished, place cooked garlic and onion in a blender or Vitamixer with vegetable broth and blend until soup reaches desired consistency. Pour soup into a bowl and squeeze lemon juice over top.

Optional: Top with roasted pumpkin seeds

Ginger Vegetable Stir Fry

INGREDIENTS

Add 1 head of cauliflower,
2 tsp of tahini,
Handful of broccoli florets,
½ pint of mushrooms,
2 tbsp. sesame oil, unrefined
1 bell pepper, chopped
1 white onion, chopped
3 garlic cloves, chopped
2 carrots, chopped
2 celery stalks, chopped
1" nub fresh ginger
4 tbsp. tamari or Bragg's Aminos
½ tsp garlic powder
½ tsp onion powder
Sesame seeds as garnish

DIRECTIONS

Add cauliflower florets into a blender or Vitamixer and pulse it until it is a rice consistency. Heat ghee to a medium heat and then saute the cauliflower rice for 5 minutes. Place to the side in a large bowl. Sauté onion and garlic in sesame oil. Add bell pepper, carrots, broccoli, mushrooms, and celery and sauté until tender.

Peel and shave fresh ginger and add to stir-fry.

Add tamari, tahini, garlic powder, and onion powder to the stir fry and stir until fully coated. Once fully coated add to the cauliflower rice and sprinkle sesame seeds over top.

INGREDIENTS

4 chicken breasts

1 tsp cinnamon

¾ tsp paprika

½ tsp cumin

½ tsp curry seasoning

½" nib fresh ginger

1 garlic clove

1 tsp Himalayan salt

1 tsp pepper

Olive oil

Coconut oil

Grated onion (using a microplane)

1/3 cup chicken broth

2 tbsp. raw honey

Handful of raisins

Handful of pistachios

DIRECTIONS

Prep: Preheat oven to 350 degrees.

Mix cinnamon, turmeric, paprika, curry powder, cumin, fresh ginger, chopped garlic, salt, and pepper in olive oil for marinade. Place chicken in marinade overnight.

Directions:
Heat coconut oil then add one grated onion and cook until tender.
Add chicken and cook for 7 minutes, then finish cooking it in the oven for 25 minutes.

In a separate bowl, put organic chicken broth, honey, a handful of raisins, and pistachios.
Mix ingredients together well.

Pour sauce over top cooked chicken and serve.

INGREDIENTS

1 ½ lbs fresh wild salmon filets
(with skin)

2 stalks of green onions

3 tbsp. Dijon mustard

3 garlic cloves, crushed

1 ½ tbsp. maple syrup or raw honey

Sea salt and black pepper to taste

DIRECTIONS

Preheat oven to 375 degrees.

In a blender or Vitamixer blend Dijon mustard, salt, pepper, maple syrup or raw honey, and garlic.

Place salmon on a baking sheet and drizzle blended Dijon mixture over top. Bake in oven for 25 minutes. Garnish with green onion before serving.

INGREDIENTS

1 ½ lbs. ground lamb

2 large sweet potatoes, chopped

2 celery stalks, thinly sliced

2 carrots, thinly sliced

1 white onion, thinly sliced

3 garlic cloves, minced

1 cup bone broth

2 tbsp. fresh parsley, chopped

1 tsp ground cinnamon

2 tsp ground cumin

1tsp. coriander

1 tbsp. extra-virgin olive oil

Sea salt and fresh ground pepper to taste

DIRECTIONS

Preheat oven to 350 degrees.

Heat ghee in a saute pan to a medium heat to brown the ground lamb. After the lamb is cooked add it to a large bowl. Then add the celery, carrots, and onion, and mix together. Add all of the spices to the bowl. Mix together until all ingredients are well combined.

Slice sweet potatoes like chips and place to the side. Drizzle the olive oil in a Dutch oven or Pyrex and place half of the sweet potatoes in a layer on the bottom. Place the lamb mixture over top the sweet potatoes then add a layer of the remaining sweet potatoes on top. Drizzle olive oil over top of the sweet potatoes and cook in the oven for 1 hour.

INGREDIENTS

3 tbsp. of capers

6 sundried tomatoes

2 pepperoncini's

Juice from 1 lemon

¼ cup of olive oil

4 sprigs parsley

1 anchovy sardine filet

2 garlic cloves

DIRECTIONS

Preheat oven to 400 degrees.

Drizzle olive oil into a Pyrex bake pan. Place thinly sliced chicken cutlets into the pan and top with a drizzle of olive oil, salt, and pepper. Place the sundried tomatoes, pepperoncini's, garlic, lemon, parsley, capers, olive oil, and sardines into a blender or Vitamixer. Blend at low to chop into a chutney/salsa. Top the chicken with the chutney and serve.

INGREDIENTS

2-3 lbs. chicken breasts sliced thin

½ cup coconut flour

1 cup of Raw coconut shreds, fine

2-3 eggs

3 tsp of Grass-fed Ghee (may need more)

Sea salt + Pepper to taste

DIRECTIONS

Heat 3tsp of ghee to medium heat in a sauté pan. As you cook the cutlets, may need more ghee. Place the coconut shred into a blender or food processor to make fine.

In a small bowl, whisk 2 eggs. On a plate add coconut flour and mix with salt and pepper. Add shredded coconut to a separate plate. Coat the chicken with the coconut flour mixture. Dip chicken in whisked eggs then coat with coconut shreds.

Place chicken cutlet into ghee and sauté until brown, about 2-3 minutes on each side.

INGREDIENTS

1 rutabaga, peeled and chopped into cubes

1 medium onion, chopped

1 fennel bulb, chopped

4 oz. shiitake mushrooms, chopped

6-8 oz. crimini mushrooms, chopped

2 cloves roasted garlic

3 cups vegetable broth

1 tsp rosemary

¾ tsp tarragon

2 tbsp. olive oil

Juice from ½ lemon

Salt and pepper to taste

DIRECTIONS

Preheat oven to 400 degrees.

Line a baking pan with parchment paper to place rutabaga cubes and 3 garlic cloves on top. Season rutabaga and garlic with salt and pepper and bake for 1 hour, or until tender.

In a large sauté pan, add olive oil, onions, fennel, salt, and pepper, and cook covered on a medium-low heat for 15 minutes.

Add shiitake mushrooms, crimini mushrooms, rosemary, tarragon, and lemon juice to sauté pan and sauté for another 20 minutes, uncovered. If mixture becomes dry, add a small amount of vegetable broth. Cook until mushrooms, onions, and fennel are all browned.

TIP: You can add more vegetable broth if you want to create a "sauce"

When the rutabagas are finished cooking, place them in a blender or Vitamixer with roasted garlic cloves and 2 cups of vegetable broth. Blend until it reaches your desired smoothness.

TIP: Be careful when blending hot ingredients. They can expand quickly when the blender is turned on, so make sure the lid is securely sealed.

Place pureed rutabaga mixture into a bowl and add sautéed vegetables on top.

INGREDIENTS

1 lb. ground turkey

1.5 lbs. ground veal

1 onion

8 garlic cloves, crushed

5 leaves fresh sage

10 leaves fresh basil

2 tsp fresh oregano

1 tsp celery seeds

Salt and pepper to taste

DIRECTIONS

Prep: Prepare the Mustard Mint sauce in "Sauces & Dressings Section".

Preheat oven to 385 degrees.

In a large bowl mix together all ingredients. Place mixture into a bread pan greased with ghee and cook for 40 minutes.

Remove from pan and slice. Pour mustard mint sauce over meatloaf before serving.

INGREDIENTS

2 lbs. short ribs

¼ cup organic taco seasoning

1 tsp black pepper

1 tsp cumin

1 tsp Himalayan salt

1 quart bone broth

½ white onion, chopped

3 garlic cloves, crushed

1 handful fresh cilantro, chopped

Butter lettuce cups

1 avocado, sliced

DIRECTIONS

Prep: Radish and Fennel Salsa from the Snacks Section

Place short ribs, taco seasoning, cumin, salt, pepper, onion, garlic and broth into a crockpot on low and cook for 8-10 hours.

When finished cooking, remove short ribs from crockpot and pull the meat from the bone.

Add desired amount of short ribs onto lettuce cups and top with fresh chopped cilantro, avocado, and the radish salsa.

Chicken with an Caper Olive Tapenade

INGREDIENTS

3lbs of Organic Chicken Breast

2 anchovy filets (jarred)

½ cup Kalamata olives

¼ cup capers

8 sprigs fresh parsley

6 leaves fresh basil

1 lemon for juice

Fresh ground pepper

Sea Salt

¼ cup olive oil

DIRECTIONS

Pre-heat the oven to 375F. Place the chicken onto a greased bake pan, season with salt and pepper before placing in the oven. Place into the oven for 15 minutes or until cooked.

In a food processer, add anchovies, olives, capers, parsley, and basil. Squeeze the juice from the lemon into the processor then add the lemon halves, without the rinds. Season mixture with salt and pepper and pulse to combine. While the motor is running slowly add the olive oil and continue blending until emulsified. Pour the mixture over roasted chicken.

Side Dishes

INGREDIENTS

6 basil leaves

6 cilantro sprigs

6 parsley sprigs

½ jar of Capers

2 lbs. black, blue, or purple potatoes

1 tbsp. Dijon mustard

2-4 anchovy filets (jarred), chopped

1 celery stalk

Olive oil

Juice from ½ lemon

3 garlic cloves

Truffle salt or Himalayan Salt

Fresh ground pepper

Crushed red pepper

DIRECTIONS

Pre-heat oven to 375 degrees.

Chop potatoes into cubes and place onto a baking sheet. Drizzle with olive oil, salt, and pepper and bake until potatoes are soft.

Remove leaves from celery and then chop the leaves into medium sized pieces and place into a bowl.

Place 2-4 anchovy filets, cilantro, parsley, basil, lemon juice, garlic, Dijon mustard, and spices into a blender.

Pour blended mixture over the cooked potatoes and garnish with capers and celery leaves.

INGREDIENTS

1 head of broccoli

1 garlic clove

2-3 anchovy filets (jarred)

2 sprigs of fresh rosemary

Red pepper flakes

¼ cup of Olive oil

Juice from ½ lemon

Salt

Pepper

DIRECTIONS

Preheat oven to 375 degrees.

Chop broccoli into florets; peel and slice the stems. Place the broccoli into a sauté pan with olive oil, salt, and pepper. Sauté for 5-7 minutes.

Place the anchovies, rosemary, garlic, olive oil, and lemon juice into a blender or food processor and blend until smooth. Pour the blended mixture over top of the cooked broccoli.

INGREDIENTS

1 bundle broccoli rabe

2 tbsp. olive oil

3 garlic cloves, crushed

Juice from ¼ lemon

Salt and pepper to taste

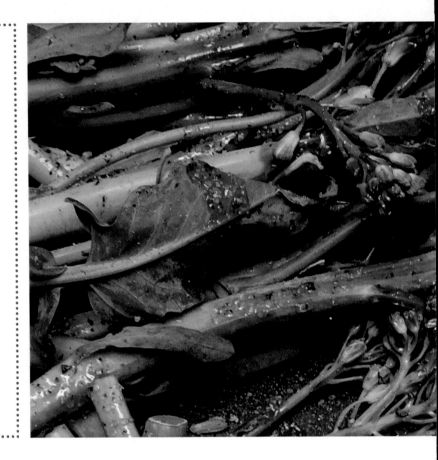

DIRECTIONS

In a sauté pan, over a medium heat, heat olive oil. Add garlic and sauté for 1-2 minutes.

Add broccoli rabe, lemon juice, salt, and pepper. Cook for 5-7 minutes or until tender, but still firm. Do not cook until soft.

INGREDIENTS

Bushel of kale

1/4 cup nutritional yeast

Juice from 1 lemon

¼ cup olive oil

1 tsp apple cider vinegar

1 tsp truffle salt or sea salt

DIRECTIONS

Rip kale leaves from the stem and place into a bowl. In a large mixing bowl massage dry kale with olive oil, making sure all leaves are covered. If you washed your kale, make sure it is dry before massaging since oil and water don't mix.

Add nutritional yeast, lemon juice, apple cider vinegar, and truffle salt. Toss until well mixed and serve.

INGREDIENTS

1 rutabaga, peeled

1 purple yam, peeled

1 sweet potato, peeled

2 tbsp. coconut oil

1 tsp Himalayan salt

1 tsp fresh ground pepper

¾ tsp thyme

¾ tsp oregano

DIRECTIONS

Preheat oven to 400 degrees.

Chop rutabaga, purple yam, and sweet potato into "fries".

On a baking sheet, melt coconut oil and place the fries on the baking sheet. Season fries with all seasonings and bake for 45 minutes.

INGREDIENTS

1 head broccoli, chopped into florets

½ white onion, finely chopped

4 garlic cloves, minced

1 cup nutritional yeast

½ cup bone broth

2 tbsp. ghee

½ tsp Himalayan salt

¾ tsp fresh ground pepper

2 green onions, chopped for garnish

1 tsp. turmeric

DIRECTIONS

Heat ghee in the sauté pan on medium heat. Add onion and garlic and sauté for 3 minutes, until garlic and onion are tender.

Add broccoli, salt, and pepper to sauté pan and cook for 2-3 minutes. Place the broccoli into a bowl.

Add 1 cup of nutritional yeast and ¼ cup bone broth to the pan and stir, to create "cheese" sauce. Add the spices and cook for another minute or until thick. Pour the sauce over top of the broccoli and garnish with chopped green onion.

INGREDIENTS

¾ lb. sunchokes aka Jerusalem Artichokes, sliced

¾ lb. brussels sprouts, sliced

¼ onion, sliced

3 garlic cloves, chopped

2 tbsp. coconut oil

½ cup vegetable broth

Juice from ½ lemon

Salt and pepper to taste

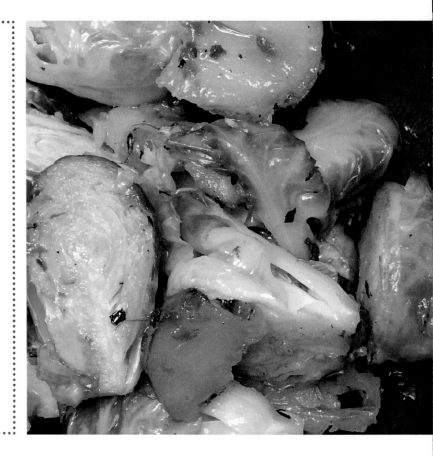

DIRECTIONS

In a sauté pan, over medium heat, melt coconut oil. Add onion and garlic and sauté for 3-4 minutes.

Add sunchokes, brussels sprouts, and vegetable broth and sauté for 10-15 minutes.

Cover and cook for another 5 minutes or until sunchokes and brussels sprouts are browned and tender. Add lemon juice.

Rutabaga Mash

INGREDIENTS

1 large rutabaga, peeled and cubed

½ large white onion, chopped

3 cloves of garlic, peeled

½ cup of bone broth

Salt and Pepper to taste

DIRECTIONS

Preheat the oven to 375F.

Grease a bake pan with ghee. Place the chopped onion, rutabaga, and garlic cloves onto the bake pan. Drizzle with olive oil and season with salt and pepper. Bake until tender. Place the contents into a food processor or Vitamixer with the bone broth. Blend until smooth.

Desserts

INGREDIENTS

¼ cup chia seeds

¼ cup raw coconut

Handful raw cashews

Cinnamon

4 dried dates

½ cup coconut milk

¼ tsp organic vanilla extract

DIRECTIONS

Mix chia seeds and raw coconut in a small bowl.

Blend cashews, cinnamon, coconut milk, dried dates, and vanilla extract in a blender or Vitamixer.

Pour blended mixture into bowl with chia seeds and coconut and stir. Wait a few minutes and then stir mixture again (you will notice the chia seeds starting to take on a gelatinous texture). Wait and stir again. Wait a few minutes and stir one more time and then place the pudding into the refrigerator for 15-20 minutes.

Can be served with berries, cacao nibs, or carob chips.

Banana Nut Bites

INGREDIENTS

4 ripe bananas

1 tsp Coconut oil

¼ cup of carob chips (optional)

1 egg

2 tbsp. Grade B maple syrup

2 tsp almond butter

¼ cup macadamia nuts or cashews, chopped

2 tsp of Cinnamon

½ tsp Ground cloves

1/2 cup coconut flour

3 tbsp. coconut milk

3 tbsp of shredded coconut

DIRECTIONS

Preheat oven to 375 degrees.

In a bowl, mash together the bananas with a fork. Once mashed, add carob chips, maple syrup, tahini or almond butter, coconut, nuts, a dash of cinnamon, a dash of cloves, coconut milk, and flour. Mix together well (if mixture is too thin add more flour).

Coat a cupcake tray with coconut oil and place a dollop of the mixture in each cupcake holder. Bake for 20-30 minutes, or until firm.

INGREDIENTS

2 cups shredded zucchini

1 cup almond butter

1 ½ cup dark chocolate chips

1 egg

1/3 cup raw honey

¼ cup applesauce

2 tsp vanilla extract

3 tbsp. cacao powder

1 tsp baking powder

DIRECTIONS

Preheat oven to 350 degrees.

In a food processor, combine all ingredients and process.

Pour brownie mixture into a greased or parchment paper lined baking pan. Place in the oven and bake for 45 minutes.

Let brownies cool before cutting and removing from the pan.

Snacks

INGREDIENTS

½ red onion, chopped

1 pint cherry tomatoes, chopped

3 garlic cloves, chopped

10 leaves fresh basil, chopped

Juice from ½ lemon

3 tbsp. olive oil

1 tbsp. red wine vinegar

Himalayan salt

Fresh ground pepper

DIRECTIONS

Place red onion, tomatoes, garlic, and fresh basil into a mixing bowl.

Add a few tablespoons of olive oil, 1 tbsp. of red wine vinegar, and a splash of lemon juice to mixture. Season with salt and pepper.

Radish and Fennel Salsa

INGREDIENTS

4 radishes, sliced thin

2 celery stalks, sliced thin

1 fennel bulb, sliced thin

3 tbsp. olive oil

1 tsp red wine vinegar

Juice from ½ lemon

Salt and pepper to taste

TIP: Use a mandolin, at ¼" setting, to get the best results when slicing vegetables.

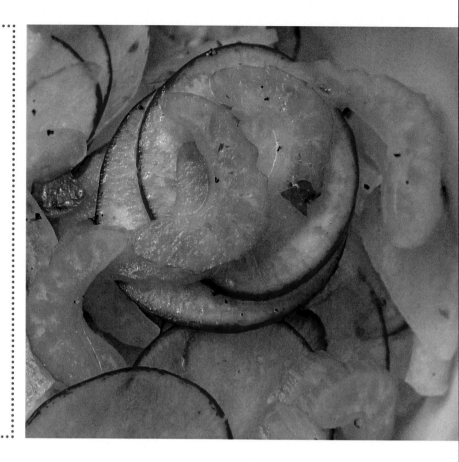

DIRECTIONS

Place radishes, celery, and fennel into a bowl and add red wine vinegar, olive oil, lemon, salt, and pepper. Mix until all vegetables are fully coated.

INGREDIENTS

2 zucchini, chopped

½ cup plain goat yogurt

2 garlic cloves, chopped

2 sprigs of mint

Juice of ½ lemon

Salt

Pepper

1 tsp of coriander

DIRECTIONS

Heat olive oil to a medium heat in a sauté pan. In a sauté pan, sauté zucchini and garlic with olive oil until tender. Add cooked zucchini and garlic to a food processor to blend.

Place mixture into a bowl adding goat yogurt, lemon juice, and mint. Season to your liking. Mix well.

Grilled Mango, Prosciutto, and Mint

INGREDIENTS

3 mangoes , sliced

12 slices of Prosciutto

12 Mint leaves

DIRECTIONS

Preheat grill.

Place one mint leaf on top of each mango slice then wrap it with 1 slice of prosciutto.

Grill for 1-3 minutes on each side.

Sauces & Dressings

Parsley Lemon

INGREDIENTS

½ Lemon

1 clove garlic

½ handful of Parsley

1/3 Cup of Braggs Olive Oil

Himalayan Salt

Ground Pepper

DIRECTIONS

Place contents into a food processor or Vitamixer and blend until smooth.

Citrus Dressing

INGREDIENTS

1 tbsp. extra-virgin olive oil

2 tbsp. fresh squeezed orange juice

2 tsp red wine vinegar

½ tsp orange zest

½ tsp Dijon mustard

Sea salt and black pepper to taste

DIRECTIONS

To make dressing – in a small bowl, combine all ingredients for the dressing and whisk until smooth.

Cilantro Lime

INGREDIENTS

½ Lime

1 clove garlic

½ of Handful of Cilantro

1/3 Cup of Braggs Olive Oil

Himalayan Salt

Ground Pepper

DIRECTIONS

Place contents into a food processor or Vitamixer and blend until smooth.

Anchovy Vinaigrette

INGREDIENTS

1 head of garlic

3 anchovy filets (jarred)

6 sprigs parsley

3 tbsp. red wine vinegar

1 lemon

1 tbsp. Dijon mustard

¼ tsp crushed red pepper flakes

1/3 cup olive oil

Salt

Fresh ground pepper

DIRECTIONS

Place contents into a food processor or Vitamixer and blend until smooth.

Chimichurri Pesto Sauce

INGREDIENTS

Handful fresh basil

Handful fresh cilantro

Handful fresh parsley

2 garlic cloves

½ lemon, without the rinds

¼ cup olive oil

Salt

Pepper

DIRECTIONS

Place contents into a food processor or Vitamixer and blend until smooth. Add water if mixture is too thick.

Artichoke Pesto Sauce

INGREDIENTS

1 jar artichokes in water

3 tbsp. olive oil

1 tsp salt

¼ lemon, peeled away from the rind

1 tsp fresh parsley

1 garlic clove

DIRECTIONS

Place all ingredients into a food processor or Vitamixer and pulse into a chunky pesto.

Mustard Mint Sauce

INGREDIENTS

1 garlic clove

1 tsp red wine vinegar

¼ cup Dijon mustard

4 tbsp. olive oil

½ tsp horseradish

2-3 tbsp. maple syrup

10 mint leaves

¼ tsp salt

½ tsp fresh ground pepper

DIRECTIONS

Place all ingredients into a food processor or Vitamixer and blend until smooth.

CHAPTER 02

Autoimmune & Anti-Inflammatory Recipes

Inflammation is a major part of an overactive immune system. Remove inflammatory and reactive foods to promote healing of the gut and manage autoimmunity.

Autoimmune Conditions and Inflammatory Conditions:

+ Psoriasis
+ Sjogren's
+ Rheumatoid Arthritis
+ Diabetes Type I
+ Hashimotos
+ Lupus
+ Graves
+ Multiple Sclerosis
+ Celiac
+ Crohns
+ IBS
+ Ulcerative Colitis
+ High Blood Pressure
+ Fibromyalgia
+ Depressed Immune System

What does it look like?

+ Constipation
+ Diarrhea
+ Bloating
+ Gas
+ Burping
+ Indigestion
+ Chronic Fatigue
+ Unexplainable Weight Gain or Weight Loss
+ Chronic Pain
+ Achy Joints
+ Headaches

Eat It:

+ Vitamin K2 Rich Foods: Goat's Milk Yogurt, Egg Yolks, Fermented Foods

+ Probiotic Rich Foods: Goat's Milk Yogurt, Raw Sauerkraut, Kimchi

+ High Quality Fats: Olive Oil, Coconut Oil, Grass Fed Ghee, Pasture Raised Grass Fed Butter

+ Quality Pasture Raised Chicken

+ Grass Fed Grass Finished Red Meats: Steak, Venison, Lamb, Duck, Bison

+ Fish: White Fish: Flounder, Mahi Mahi, Sea Bass, Striped Bass, Rockfish, Flounder, Scrod

+ Organ Meats: Liver, Thymus Gland (aka Sweet Breads), Bone Marrow

+ Chicken or Beef Bone Marrow Broth

Don't Eat It:

Inflammatory Foods:

+ Oatmeal
+ Grains: Oats, Quinoa, Brown Rice, Wild Rice, Buckwheat, Amaranth, Millet, Barley, Spelt, Kamut
+ Wheat & Wheat Gluten
+ Nightshades: Tomatoes, Eggplant, Peppers, and White Potatoes (Sweet Potatoes are the Exception)
+ Shellfish especially Shrimp
+ Asparagus
+ Nuts
+ Seeds
+ Fruit: Limit to 1 Serving Per Day ie. 1 Cup of Berries or ½ Banana
+ Legumes: Black Beans, Garbanzo Beans, Cannellini Beans, Kidney Beans, and Peanuts
+ Cow's Milk Dairy
+ Refined Sugars & Artificial Sweeteners
+ Corn
+ Soy: Soy Milk, Soy Oil, Tofu, or Tempeh

Hashimoto's and Graves:

+ Cruciferous Vegetables must only be consumed cooked: Cauliflower, Broccoli, Bok Choy, Cabbage, Brussel Sprouts, Wasabi, Kohlrabi, Collard Greens, Turnips, Kale, Swiss Chard.

+ No Iodine rich Foods such as Kelp, Sea Veggies, & Shellfish.

Breakfast Time

INGREDIENTS

Avocado(s), sliced

2 eggs (per avocado)

1 tbsp. vinegar

Himalayan salt

Pepper

Dash of Cayenne

Dash of turmeric

DIRECTIONS

Fill a small saucepan with 2-3 inches of water and place on a medium-high heat. Add vinegar to water and allow to come to a slow boil.

In a bowl, crack one egg, making sure that the yolk remains intact.

When water begins to boil, take a spoon and start to stir water to create a "whirlpool" in the water. Gently drop egg into the center of the water. The spinning motion and the vinegar will help the egg white stay together. Cook one egg at a time for 3-4 minutes, until egg whites are firm but still have a bouncy resistance when touched with a spoon.

Using a slotted spoon, remove egg from water.

Put 3-4 slices of avocado on a plate and top with the poached egg. Season with salt, pepper, turmeric, and cayenne to your liking.

INGREDIENTS

2 large sweet potatoes or yams, chopped

4 garlic cloves, chopped

1 large onion, chopped

2-3 andouille chicken sausage, chopped

1 cup vegetable broth

Himalayan salt

Fresh ground pepper

Turmeric

Cayenne

3 tbsp. of chipotle seasoning

DIRECTIONS

Peel and chop sweet potatoes into small cubes. Slice the chicken sausage down the center and then slice into small pieces. In a sauté pan, sauté garlic, onions, and sausage in olive oil until tender. Add sweet potatoes and ½ cup of vegetable broth. Cook with the lid on to soften potatoes. Add more broth if needed, to soften sweet potatoes.

Season to your liking with Himalayan salt, pepper, garlic powder, turmeric, cayenne, and chipotle seasoning. The chipotle is the key ingredient.

INGREDIENTS

½ onion

1lb. short ribs, cooked in crockpot

2 golden beets

2 garlic cloves, crushed

2 tsp of Bone Broth or Veggie Broth

2 tsp ghee

Salt and pepper to taste

DIRECTIONS

Prep: Cook the short ribs in bone broth in a crockpot overnight for 8-10 hours on low.

Directions:
In a sauté pan heat the ghee over a medium heat.

Place the onion, garlic, beets, salt, and pepper in the sauté pan to cook until tender. ADD bone broth and cook with the lid on to soften the beets.

Add the short ribs in the last minute of cooking in order to heat them, since they are already cooked. Serve with eggs is desired.

INGREDIENTS

2 eggs

3 tsp of ghee

1 leek, sliced

1 bunch of asparagus

1 garlic clove, minced

2-3 tbsp. fresh chives, minced (optional)

Sea salt

Fresh ground pepper

DIRECTIONS

Preheat oven to 400 degrees.

Place asparagus and leeks onto a bake pan with ghee. Bake for 10-12 minutes or until firm but tender.

Heat ghee in a skillet and then add the garlic. After one minute, add the eggs to the skillet. Cook to your liking. Garnish with fresh chives and serve over the asparagus and leeks.

INGREDIENTS

8 oz. heritage bacon, cubed

8 oz. fresh crimini mushrooms, sliced

½ white onion, finely chopped

2 garlic cloves, minced

1 tsp ghee

¼ tsp Himalayan salt

¾ tsp fresh ground pepper

4 eggs, cracked into individual
ramekins for poaching

1 tsp. vinegar

1 tsp parsley, chopped (for garnish)

Olive oil (for garnish)

DIRECTIONS

In a medium saucepan, over a medium-high heat, pour about 3 inches of water and bring to a boil for the poached egg.

While waiting for water to boil, in a sauté pan heat ghee on a medium-high heat, then add chopped bacon and cook for 5-6 minutes, until bacon is lightly crisp. Remove the bacon but leave the bacon drippings in the pan.

Add onion, garlic, mushrooms, salt, and pepper to the sauté pan and cook for about 8 minutes. The onions should be soft and the mushrooms browned. Remove pan from heat and add the bacon back in.

When the water comes to a slow boil add the vinegar. Crack the eggs into individual ramekins to ensure the yolk doesn't break into the boiling water, and no shells are present. Stir the boiling water to create a "whirlpool" and drop one egg into the center of the saucepan. The vinegar and whirlpool will help to keep the egg whites together so you will have a whole poached egg.

Cook for 4 minutes, or until the whites are just barely firm. Remove from the water with a slotted spoon. Repeat process with the 3 remaining eggs.

To serve, put desired amount of bacon mixture on a plate and top with one poached egg. Drizzle a small amount of olive oil over top and garnish with chopped parsley.

Lunch
Time

INGREDIENTS

1-2 lb. chicken cutlets

¼ cup organic taco seasoning

1 tsp cumin

1 tsp Himalayan salt

1 quart chicken broth or bone broth

½ white onion, chopped

2 tsp of green onion

3 garlic cloves, crushed

1 handful fresh cilantro, chopped

1 avocado, chopped

Butter lettuce cups or Swiss chard

DIRECTIONS

Chop chicken cutlets into cubes. Place chicken, garlic, onion, seasonings, and broth into the crockpot on low for 8-10 hours. Make sure there is enough broth so the chicken does not dry out.

When finished, place chicken into the lettuce boats and top with chopped cilantro, green onion, and fresh avocado.

INGREDIENTS

3 medium/large beets, thinly sliced

4 celery stalks, thinly sliced

Juice of 2 lemons

2 tbsp. apple cider vinegar

3 tbsp. olive oil

Salt and pepper to taste

DIRECTIONS

TIP: Use Mandoline if possible

Slice beets and celery with a mandolin, if possible. Otherwise, you can slice the beets and celery as thin as possible using a knife. Place sliced beets and celery into a mixing bowl. Add lemon juice, olive oil, apple cider vinegar, salt, and pepper. Allow mixture to marinate for an hour, or you can eat immediately if you prefer more firm veggies.

INGREDIENTS

2 celery stalks, chopped

½ red onion, chopped

3 carrots, chopped

6 hard-boiled eggs

2 tbsp. Dijon mustard

1 garlic clove, crushed

3 tbsp. olive oil

Juice from ½ lemon

Salt and pepper to taste

DIRECTIONS

To hard boil eggs: place 6 eggs into a stock pot and cover with water. Place the pot onto the stove and heat at a medium to high heat. Allow the water to come to a boil, keep at a boil for 2 minutes. Remove from the heat, dump the hot water and run cold water over the eggs. After they are cool, peel them and place them into a bowl. Use a fork and knife to chop the eggs.

Chop the onion, carrots, celery and add to a bowl. Add the remaining ingredients into a bowl, mix, and season as desired.

INGREDIENTS

<u>Lamb Burger Ingredients:</u>
2 lbs. ground lamb
¼ cup Moroccan seasoning: see spice section to make your own Moroccan seasoning
2 tsp Himalayan salt
2 tsp garlic powder
Handful fresh parsley, chopped

<u>Tzatziki Ingredients:</u>
2 cups plain goat yogurt
1 cucumber, chopped
3 tbsp. fresh dill or dry dill
2 garlic cloves, crushed
2 tsp salt
Fresh ground pepper
Juice from ½ lemon

DIRECTIONS

Pre-heat oven to 375 degrees

Directions for Burgers:
Mix spices and ground lamb and make into burgers. Bake for 25 minutes.

Directions for Tzatziki:
In a bowl mix goat yogurt, chopped cucumber, dill, lemon juice, and all spices.

When burgers are finished, place a spoonful of Goat Tzatziki on top of each and serve.

INGREDIENTS

2- 1lb. tuna steak

2 avocados

Juice from ½ lemon

2 green onions, minced (keep some of the green part aside)

1 garlic clove, minced

1 tbsp. ground paprika

½ cup olive oil

2 tbsp. ghee or butter

Sea salt and fresh ground pepper to taste

DIRECTIONS

In a skillet placed over a medium/high heat, heat the butter or ghee until hot. Add the tuna steak to the skillet and cook each side for 4-5 minutes. When the tuna steak is fully cooked let it rest for about 10 minutes.

In a bowl combine garlic, lemon juice, green onions, and olive oil. Season with sea salt and black pepper to taste.

Gently remove the pit from both avocados. Slice the avocado and remove it from the skin. Top the tuna steak with the green onion mixture and avocado slices.

INGREDIENTS

2 lb. ground chicken

1 egg yolk

5-6 garlic cloves, minced

¼ white onion, chopped

8 leaves fresh basil, chopped

1 handful fresh parsley, chopped

2 tsp salt

2 tsp pepper

½ tsp garlic powder

½ tsp onion powder

3 tbsp. olive oil

DIRECTIONS

In a large mixing bowl, combine all ingredients, except olive oil. Once mixed, form into 2" diameter meatballs; should make approximately 20 meatballs.

In a pot, over medium heat, add olive oil. Place meatballs in pot and brown on both sides. When cooked, remove meatballs from pot and place on paper towel to remove excess olive oil. If you choose to bake the meatballs, you can line a bake sheet with parchment paper. Drizzle olive oil onto the parchment paper and place meatballs onto the pan for baking. Bake at 375F for 30 minutes. Serve with spaghetti squash.

INGREDIENTS

2 lb. ground chicken

1 handful fresh basil

1 tsp lemon juice

4 cloves garlic, crushed

1 handful parsley

1 egg yolk

Grass fed butter

1 tsp buckwheat flour (optional)

DIRECTIONS

Preheat oven to 375 degrees.

In a bowl, add ground chicken, salt, pepper, garlic powder, chopped basil, chopped parsley, and the egg yolk. Add lemon juice and crushed garlic then mix all ingredients. (If you are having a hard time forming patties add a small amount of buckwheat flour to mixture.) Make sure to leave some of the meat mixture to the side.

Once all the burgers are formed, make an indentation in the middle of each one and place 1 teaspoon of grass fed butter in each. Add more of the meat mixture over top in order to seal in the butter. Bake burgers in the oven for 30 minutes.

INGREDIENTS

1 lb. brussel sprouts, sliced

½ head of Radicchio

¼ red onion, thinly sliced

¼ cup olive oil

Juice from 2 lemons

2 garlic cloves, crushed

4-6 tbsp. red wine vinegar

Himalayan salt

Fresh ground pepper

Truffle salt

DIRECTIONS

TIP: Use Mandoline if possible

Preferably, slice the Brussel sprouts and Onion with a mandolin. Otherwise slice as thin as possible. Slice the radicchio with a knife. Put sliced brussel sprouts, radicchio, and red onion in a bowl.

In a Vitamixer or blender, add olive oil, garlic, lemon, red wine vinegar, pepper, and Himalayan salt and blend.

Add mixture into bowl, coating the brussel sprouts and onion. Let marinate for 15 minutes.

Garnish with truffle salt.

INGREDIENTS

2 salmon filets (1 lb.)

4 tsp plain goat yogurt

1 tsp Dijon mustard

3 tsp fresh dill

1 garlic clove, crushed

2 tbsp. green onion

1 tbsp. capers (optional)

Salt and pepper to taste

DIRECTIONS

Preheat oven to 375 degrees.

Coat baking sheet with olive oil and place salmon filets on pan. Season with salt and pepper and cook in the oven for 15-20 minutes. In a bowl, add the yogurt, mustard, dill, spices, garlic and mix until smooth. Then add the capers and green onion.

After filets are cooked, add the salmon to a bowl and use a fork to break it up. Then add the salmon to the yogurt mixture and mix together well.

Dinner Time

INGREDIENTS

1 lb. grass fed/grass finished short ribs, brisket, or lamb

6 carrots, chopped

1 leek or onion, chopped

4 garlic cloves, chopped

2 tsp apple cider vinegar

2-3 cups of bone broth

2 tsp Himalayan salt

1 tsp fresh ground pepper

1 tsp turmeric

½ tsp cayenne

2 tsp garlic powder

2 tsp onion powder

DIRECTIONS

Place all ingredients into crockpot and cook for 8-10 hours.

Serve with sweet potato mash or rutabaga mash.

INGREDIENTS

4 links chicken apple sausage, chopped into 1" pieces

1 fennel bulb, thinly sliced

1 tsp coconut oil

Himalayan Salt

Pepper to taste

DIRECTIONS

Prep: Prepare Garlic Lemon Vinaigrette using recipe from Sauces and Dressings section.

vIn a sauté pan, over medium heat, melt coconut oil and then add sausage. Sauté until golden brown, then remove from pan and place in a separate bowl.

In the same sauté pan add fennel, salt, and pepper, and sauté for 8-10 minutes, or until browned and tender.

Remove fennel from pan and place in bowl with sausage. Pour Garlic Lemon Vinaigrette sauce over sausage and fennel and mix well.

INGREDIENTS

3 wild cod filets
½ white onion
6 garlic cloves, chopped
¾ cup Kalamata olives
1 cup jarred artichoke hearts
¼ cup juice from artichoke hearts
3 tbsp. jarred capers
2 tsp juice from capers
1 cup white cooking wine
Juice from ½ lemon
2 tbsp. olive oil
2 tbsp. grass fed butter
6 fresh sardine filets (optional)
Fresh parsley, for garnish
Salt and pepper to taste

DIRECTIONS

Preheat oven to 400 degrees, and place either a terra cotta pot or glass dish in oven to preheat as well.

Sauté onion and garlic with some salt and pepper in olive oil for 3-4 minutes, until tender. Add white wine and lemon juice and allow to cook for another 3-4 minutes. Add olives, artichokes, and capers and cook for another 2 minutes. Add butter and allow to melt into sauce.

Carefully remove the hot baking dish from oven and place cod filets in. Also add sardines if you choose to use them.

Pour sauce over the fish and then place into oven. Bake for 15 to 20 minutes, depending on size of cod filets. Fish will be slightly firm to the touch when finished, and sauce will be bubbly around the outside of the baking dish.

Garnish with fresh chopped parsley and serve over spaghetti squash.

INGREDIENTS

Organic beef long bones
Use 6" of bone for every ½ gallon of
water
1 large onion, chopped
3 whole carrots, chopped
2 celery stalks, chopped
4 garlic cloves
2 tsp of Apple Cider Vinegar
Himalayan sea salt
Fresh ground black pepper

DIRECTIONS

Place bones onto a bake sheet and roast at 350F for 40 minutes. Then place bones, onion, carrots, celery, garlic cloves (whole), vinegar, salt, and pepper in a crockpot and fill with filtered water. Cook for approximately 12 hours. Once fully cooked, remove vegetables and bones from crockpot and extract bone marrow out of bones while they are still warm; to do this, bang the bone on a thick wooden chopping board. The gelatinous soft tissues around the bones and the bone barrow provide the best healing remedies for the gut lining and the immune system. Puree the bone marrow until smooth and place back into broth.

INGREDIENTS

2 quarts bone broth

4-5 cloves garlic, crushed

1 white onion, chopped

3-4 carrots, peeled and chopped

3-4 celery stalks, chopped

4 small beets, peeled and chopped
(Mix of Yellow and Red)

3-4 sprigs of fresh parsley

Himalayan salt

Black pepper to taste

DIRECTIONS

Add bone broth, vegetables, and seasonings to a large stockpot. Simmer for 1 ½- 2 hours.

INGREDIENTS

4 heritage pork chops

4 tbsp. fresh dill, chopped

4 tbsp. fresh rosemary, chopped

2 celery stalks, chopped

2 tbsp. Himalayan salt

2 tbsp. fresh ground pepper

6 garlic cloves, minced

2 tsp onion powder

4 tsp olive oil

4 tsp Dijon mustard

1 tsp Braggs aminos

1 tsp Braggs apple cider vinegar

DIRECTIONS

In a mixing bowl, add all ingredients to make marinade and mix together well.

Place pork chops on a baking sheet and pour marinade over top. Rub marinade onto both sides of the pork chops until they are completely coated. Cover with tin foil and place in the refrigerator to marinate for 1-2 hours.

When finished marinating, preheat oven to 400 degrees. Bake pork chops in oven for 20-25 minutes, or until pork chops are firm to the touch.

INGREDIENTS

2 lb. tuna steak

2 tsp ghee

Salt and pepper to taste

Avocado mango salsa

DIRECTIONS

Prep: Prepare Avocado Mango Salsa using recipe from Snacks section.

Directions:

In a sauté pan, heat ghee over a medium heat. Season the tuna steak with salt and pepper then place into sauté pan. Cook for 1 minute on each side for a rare tuna steak.

Using a sharp knife, slice the tuna steak into strips. Place avocado mango salsa on top of tuna and serve.

INGREDIENTS

1 lb. pork tenderloin, chopped into 1" cubes

1 onion, chopped

Full head of cauliflower, chopped into florets

6 garlic cloves, crushed

2" nub of ginger, grated

3 eggs

Sesame oil, unrefined

2 tbsp. vegetable broth

2 tbsp. Thai basil (optional)

Salt and pepper to taste

DIRECTIONS

Add cauliflower florets into a blender or Vitamixer and pulse it until it is a rice consistency. Set to the side.

In a sauté pan, add 1tsp sesame oil and chopped pork. Cook for 10-12 minutes, or until the pork is tender.

When finished, set to the side.

In the same pan add onion, garlic, ginger, eggs, 1 tsp. sesame oil, salt, pepper, and Thai basil (optional).

Cook until eggs are firm. Place in a bowl and put it to the side.

Add cauliflower rice and vegetable broth to a sauté pan and cook for 5-7 minutes.

Add pork and sautéed mixture to pan and cook for another 5 minutes to blend flavors.

INGREDIENTS

2-3 lb. turkey breast or turkey london broil

1 fennel bulb, roughly chopped

3 celery stalks, chopped

½ large white onion, chopped

2 tsp red wine vinegar

1 cup white wine

1 cup bone broth

2 tbsp. ghee

1 tsp fresh parsley, chopped

2 tsp fresh rosemary

1 tsp thyme

Salt and pepper to taste

DIRECTIONS

Preheat conventional oven to 375 degrees.

In the dutch oven, on the stove top, melt ghee on a medium heat. Add vegetables, salt, pepper, and herbs and sauté for about 5 minutes.

Add white wine, bone broth, and vinegar and cook for another 2 minutes, stirring vegetables.

Season turkey with salt and pepper. Place the turkey into the dutch oven, with the vegetables, and cover. Place dutch oven into the conventional oven and let cook for 30-45 minutes, or until turkey reaches 165 degrees.

When finished, remove turkey from dutch oven and allow to cool for 6-8 minutes before slicing.

INGREDIENTS

1 spaghetti squash

¼ cup fresh pesto sauce

DIRECTIONS

Prep: Pesto from Sauces and Dressings section

Preheat oven to 375 degrees.

Cut the spaghetti squash in half and scoop out all of the seeds with a spoon. On a baking sheet coated with coconut oil, place both squash halves, cut side down. Bake for one hour, or until the flesh pulls away easy using a fork.

Top the spaghetti squash with the fresh pesto sauce.

INGREDIENTS

1 lb. pork tenderloin
2 tbsp. coconut oil
½ tsp sweet smoked Spanish paprika
2 tbsp. coffee grounds
¾ tsp black pepper
½ tsp cumin
3 tbsp. mustard powder
½ chipotle seasoning
¾ tsp Himalayan salt
2 tsp brown sugar
1 tsp cacao powder
½ tsp coriander
½ tsp paprika

NOTE: You can opt for a blend called Black Dust Coffee and Spice Rub made by Savory Spice Shop: 4 tbsp.

DIRECTIONS

Preheat oven to 375 degrees.

Season pork tenderloin with black dust coffee and spice rub and sweet smoked Spanish paprika. Make sure tenderloin is fully coated.
(If you are not using the seasoning blends: on a plate add all spices and mix together well, then season pork tenderloin. Make sure it is fully coated.)

In a sauté pan, melt coconut oil over a medium heat. Place pork tenderloin in pan and sear both sides for 2 minutes, or until both sides are golden brown.

Remove tenderloin from sauté pan and place on a baking sheet. Bake in oven for 12-15 minutes or until tender.

Side Dishes

INGREDIENTS

1 lb. cucumber, sliced

¼ cup goat yogurt

1 tbsp. fresh dill, finely chopped

1 tbsp. fresh chives, finely chopped

1 tbsp. white wine vinegar

Sea salt and fresh ground pepper

DIRECTIONS

In a large bowl combine goat yogurt, dill, chives, vinegar, and season to your liking with salt and pepper. Mix all ingredients well.

Add cucumber slices and stir gently until everything is combined. Serve right away or refrigerate.

INGREDIENTS

3 large yams or sweet potatoes, peeled and cubed

Fresh 2" nub of ginger, shaved

2 tbsp. fresh lime juice

Salt and pepper to taste

DIRECTIONS

Preheat oven to 375 degrees.

Coat a baking pan with coconut oil and place cubed sweet potatoes onto pan. Season to your liking and bake until tender.

When fully baked place into a bowl and mash. Add shaved ginger, lime juice, and salt. Mix thoroughly.

INGREDIENTS

2 rutabaga, peeled and sliced into ¾"
sticks

2 tbsp. coconut oil

1 tsp oregano

½ tsp thyme

Salt and pepper to taste

DIRECTIONS

Pre-heat oven to 400 degrees.

Place sliced rutabaga and seasonings onto a baking sheet and bake for about 45 minutes, turning over once. Cook until both sides are browned.

INGREDIENTS

3 large sweet potato, peeled and cubed

2 tsp of bone broth or vegetable broth

¾ tsp Himalayan salt

¾ tsp fresh ground pepper

½ tsp garlic powder

¼ tsp ground clove

¼ tsp of cinnamon

1 tsp grass fed butter

4 chives, chopped for garnish

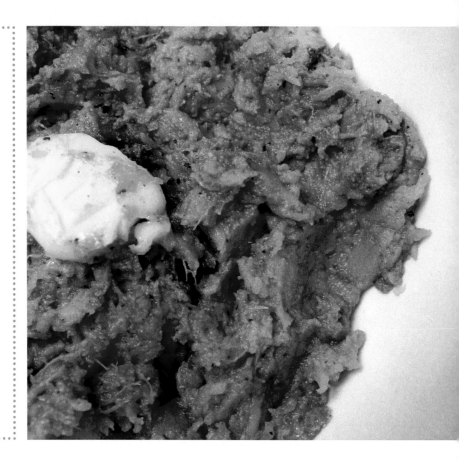

DIRECTIONS

Add 6 cups of water to a stockpot and bring to a boil. Add sweet potatoes to the pot and cook or 20 minutes, or until tender.

When the potatoes are "fork tender," strain water and add broth, butter, and spices. Mash together all of the ingredients in the pot. Add chopped chives for garnish.

INGREDIENTS

1 bundle broccolini
2 tbsp. olive oil
3 garlic cloves, crushed
Red pepper flakes
Juice from ¼ lemon
Salt and pepper to taste

DIRECTIONS

In a sauté pan, over a medium heat, heat olive oil. Add garlic and sauté for 1-2 minutes.

Add broccolini, lemon juice, salt, pepper, and a dash of red pepper flakes. Cook for 5-7 minutes or until tender, but still firm. Do not cook until soft.

INGREDIENTS

1 head cauliflower, cut into florets
2 tsp turmeric
3 tsp coconut oil, melted
Dash of cayenne
Salt and pepper to taste

DIRECTIONS

Preheat oven to 375 degrees.

Place cauliflower florets into a bowl with coconut oil and mix until cauliflower is fully coated.

Coat a baking sheet with coconut oil, place cauliflower on sheet and season with turmeric, salt, pepper, and cayenne. Bake for 20-25 minutes or until tender, but firm.

INGREDIENTS

12 oz. spinach (1 package)

2 garlic cloves, chopped

½ onion, chopped

1 tbsp. coconut oil

Salt and pepper to taste

DIRECTIONS

In a sauté pan, over medium heat, melt coconut oil. Add onion and garlic and sauté for 3 minutes.

Add spinach, salt, and pepper, and cook until the spinach has wilted.

Desserts

INGREDIENTS

Macaroon Ingredients:
2 cups of raw shredded coconut
2 egg whites, whipped
1 tsp of lemon zest
Juice from 1 lemon
½ of Vanilla Extract

Custard Ingredients:
½ cup of raw organic honey
1 tsp of lemon zest
Juice from 2 lemons
2 tbsp of grass fed ghee
3 egg yolks
1 whole egg

DIRECTIONS

Pre-heat the oven to 375F. Add shredded coconut, lemon zest, vanilla, and lemon juice to a large bowl. In a separate bowl, add 2 egg whites and whisk with a hand mixer on high until fluffy. You will fold in the egg whites into the coconut mixture. After mixed, form the dough-like mixture into balls and place onto a baking sheet lined with parchment paper. Once on the sheet, press your thumb into the center of the macaroon to make an indent for the custard. Bake at 375F for 15 minutes or until firm.

To prepare the custard, add the honey and ghee to a mixing bowl. Use the hand mixer to blend the ghee and honey together. Add the eggs/yolks to the honey and ghee mixture and continue to blend with the hand mixer until smooth. Add the lemon juice and lemon zest and blend for another few seconds. Add the custard to a sauce pan and cook on a medium heat for 10 minutes. Once the mixture starts to bubble it is finished. Add the custard to a bowl and place in the refrigerator until cooled. Scoop the custard onto the macaroons after they are cooled.

INGREDIENTS

2-3 ripe bananas
1 dried date
2 cups vanilla coconut milk
2 dashes cinnamon
1 tsp vanilla extract
1 cup chia seeds

DIRECTIONS

Blend coconut milk, vanilla extract, cinnamon, date, and bananas in a blender or Vitamixer.

Once blended, place into a large bowl and add chia seeds. Let sit for 10 minutes; mixture will form into a pudding. Add more chia to make firmer.

INGREDIENTS

4 very ripe bananas (brown/black- the riper the sweeter and the smoother the pudding will be)

1 avocado, peeled and pitted

¼ cup cacao powder

Chopped nuts (optional)

DIRECTIONS

Put all ingredients in a blender or Vitamixer and puree until smooth. Pour pudding into serving bowls and sprinkle with chopped nuts (optional).

Snacks

INGREDIENTS

3 ripe avocados, sliced

1 red onion, chopped

2 garlic cloves, chopped

1 jalapeno, chopped

Handful of cilantro, chopped

Juice of 1-2 limes

Himalayan salt

Fresh ground pepper to taste

1 tsp Taco seasoning

1 tsp Cumin

DIRECTIONS

Place sliced avocados, red onion, garlic, jalapeno, and cilantro into a mixing bowl. Add juice from 1-2 limes, and season mixture with salt, pepper, cumin, and a small amount of taco seasoning.
Mix ingredients together and enjoy!

INGREDIENTS

½ butternut squash, cut length-wise & seeded

1-2 tbsp. tahini

1 clove garlic

2 tbsp. olive oil

Juice from ½ lemon

Himalayan salt to taste

1 tsp of Hot sauce

DIRECTIONS

Preheat oven to 350 degrees.

Rub olive oil all over half of the butternut squash. Sprinkle with salt then place face down on a baking sheet. Roast for 1 hour, until very tender.

Once removed from oven, wait for squash to cool, then scoop out flesh and put into a food processor. Add olive oil, tahini, garlic, lemon juice, salt, and a dash of hot sauce. Puree until smooth. After pureed add more olive oil, salt, hot sauce, and tahini to taste.

INGREDIENTS

3 ripe avocados

2 ripe mangos

Juice from 2-3 limes

3 tbsp. olive oil

2 tbsp. fresh cilantro, finely chopped

¾ tsp salt

1 tsp pepper

¼ jalapeno, minced (optional)

DIRECTIONS

Slice the mango away from the pit and chop into cubes. Slice the avocado down the middle and twist away from the pit. Remove the pit and slice the avocado while in the skin. You can then use a spoon to scoop out the pre-cut avocado. Chop the avocados into ¾ inch cubes.

Add mangos, avocados, and all remaining ingredients into a large mixing bowl and mix ingredients together thoroughly.

Sauces & Dressings

Basil Pesto

INGREDIENTS

½ Lemon

1 clove garlic

1 large handful of Basil

1/3 Cup of Braggs Olive Oil

½ tsp Himalayan Salt

½ tsp of Ground Pepper

2 tsp of Pine nuts (optional)

DIRECTIONS

Place contents into a blender and blend for 15 seconds or until smooth.

Garlic Lemon Vinaigrette

INGREDIENTS

1-2 garlic cloves

Juice of 1 lemon

2 tsp red wine vinegar

¼ cup olive oil

½ tsp salt

½ tsp pepper

DIRECTIONS

Place contents into a blender and blend for 15 seconds or until smooth.

Pomegranate Vinaigrette

INGREDIENTS

1 garlic clove

Seeds from 1 pomegranate

2 tsp red wine vinegar

Juice from ½ of a lemon

¼ cup olive oil

1 tsp salt

1 tsp pepper

DIRECTIONS

Place contents into a blender and blend for 15 seconds or until smooth.

Strawberry Chia Basil

INGREDIENTS

5 large basil leaves

5 strawberries

2 tbsp. chia seeds

2 tsp white balsamic or red wine vinegar

1 garlic clove

1 tsp salt

1 tsp pepper

DIRECTIONS

Place contents into a blender and
blend for 15 seconds or until smooth.

....

Lemon Basil Vinaigrette

INGREDIENTS

1 handful basil

1 lemon

2 garlic cloves

¼ cup olive oil

1 tsp balsamic vinegar

1 tsp salt

1 tsp pepper

DIRECTIONS

Place contents into a blender and blend
for 15 seconds or until smooth.

THANK YOU!

There are many thank you's that go out to the amazing support team I had throughout the process of writing, cooking, preparing, photographing, staging, and losing my mind. I would like to preface that this cookbook was made in an 8' x 4' kitchen with no dishwasher.

My Love, My Man, and My Dishwasher: My amazing fiancé scrubbed every dish I flung into the sink as I trashed the kitchen to prep anywhere from 10 to 20 recipes for photographing. He was sweet enough to run out to the grocery store every time I ran out of an ingredient and poured me many glasses of wine! He is the best man I know and I am so fortunate to have his elbow grease to bring this cookbook to life.

My Bestie and Partner in Crime: I had a sizzling side kick in the kitchen through many cooking adventures. He is one of the best cooks I know and am so lucky to have his help in the kitchen. He provided inspiration, recipe ideas, and got his hands dirty while cooking by my side. I may have beat him to the punch, but I cannot wait to see his cookbook one day.

My Sister: I first need to thank her for the fancy camera she let me steal for 6 months to shoot my recipes. I thank her for her patience since every time she thought we were done collaborating recipes, I added 5 new ones to the book. She also chased me around the kitchen to scribble ingredient measurements since I hate doing that. She has been an amazing part of this process and I could not have completed this book without her.

My Photographer, My dear friend set up various shoots with me to catch my skills in action and stage some mouthwatering photos. She also edited many of the food photos. Who knows where my photos would have been without her artistic eye.

Coastal Kitchens of Belmar was kind enough to open up their top of the line kitchen to make me look super official. Only if you could see what I really cooked in.

Big thanks to our friends of **Talula's of Asbury Park** who offered their restaurant to stage some great photos. Much love to our local community for their support.

My Friends and Family aka Taste Testers: Thank you to all of my friends and family that enjoyed my recipes and shared wonderful feedback to help master my recipes

Index

Made in the USA
Middletown, DE
22 July 2016